PEER TUTORIAL INSTRUCTION

The Instructional Design Library

Volume 28

PEER TUTORIAL INSTRUCTION

William R. Endsley

Danny G. Langdon
Series Editor

Educational Technology Publications
Englewood Cliffs, New Jersey 07632

Library of Congress Cataloging in Publication Data

Endsley, William R
    Peer tutorial instruction.

    (The Instructional design library; v. 28)
    Bibliography: p.
    1. Peer-group tutoring of students. I. Title.
II. Series: Instructional design library;
v. 28.
LC41.E52   371.39'4   79-23110
ISBN 0-87778-148-6

Printed in the United States of America.

Library of Congress Catalog Card Number:
79-23110.

International Standard Book Number:
0-87778-148-6.

First Printing: March, 1980.

FOREWORD

Can peers teach one another? If so, under what circumstances, at what levels, and under what sort of relationship? Given that the answer is "yes" and that the conditions can be met, Dr. William Endsley gives us many useful insights, a practical format, and a rich set of illustrated examples from which to work.

It seems to me that there is a strong similarity between instructional designers and tutors, which will perhaps explain why tutoring (and peer tutoring, in particular) can be effective. Often as not, an instructional designer is not a subject matter expert. He or she must learn the subject through the tools he or she makes use of in analysis. Then, the subject must be communicated through development and evaluation techniques. Such a process places the technologist at a level of not quite being an expert in the subject, but also of not being a student. Thus, the technologist can communicate perhaps at a level closer to the students' needs than an expert who, in a sense, knows his or her subject *so well* that he or she assumes too much in trying to communicate it directly to students. This is the same as a peer tutor who has just learned the subject and is in a position to instruct a peer tutee who needs to learn. When the tutor is properly equipped with the tools of tutoring, in the same sense that a technologist has his or her tools of the trade, then the level of communication should be just about right.

This book can be extremely valuable in learning what these

tools of tutoring are, and what the proper relationship should be between tutor and tutee.

Danny G. Langdon
Series Editor

PREFACE

Certainly, when one finishes a product, such as *Peer Tutorial Instruction,* sincere thanks are usually extended to many. In this case, however, only three people need be specifically thanked and, thus, recognized.

The first is Danny G. Langdon for extending me the opportunity to write in *The Instructional Design Library* series. Also for his patience and understanding when my writing was seriously interrupted time after time. Second, to Grant V. Harrison for his exceptional pioneering work in structured tutoring. Many of the ideas presented in this book are the results of Harrison's original thinking and the inspiration he gave to the author while attending graduate school at Brigham Young University. The third and last person is Carol Brannan. She not only typed the manuscript twice, but also gave courteous suggestions and politely pointed out not so obvious errors in my original writing. To these people, I am indebted.

W.R.E.

CONTENTS

ABSTRACT

PEER TUTORIAL INSTRUCTION

. Peer Tutorial Instruction is an instructional system designed primarily to remediate learning and attitudinal deficiencies in problem learners. The design is flexible enough to be adapted in a large variety of subject areas, utilizing student tutors from third or fourth grade on up to college students.

There are three major factors in setting up a peer tutorial system. The first is developing the forms and procedures to be used during the tutorial sessions. The second is the judicious selection and training of peer tutors. The third consists of monitoring and evaluating the tutorial system and individual student progress.

The peer tutorial design is cost-effective. However, the most important characteristic is its ability not only to cause increased learning gains and enhance positive attitudinal growth in problem learners, but also to foster similar, yet higher level, development in the peer tutors.

PEER TUTORIAL INSTRUCTION

I.

USE

Most individualized instructional programs in our schools today demand that students work independently, read at grade level, know how to pace themselves, and demonstrate more than an average amount of self-discipline and motivation. On the other hand, these demands are too rigorous for low achievers, who are often lacking in self-confidence, motivation, ability to work alone, self-discipline, and reading skills. It is no wonder that low achievers experience higher rates of failure in typical individualized instructional systems.

The insensitivity of individualized instructional systems to low achievers often means failure to the student and eventually to the system itself. What is needed is a more specific diagnosis of the learning deficiencies in students; learning activities developed upon the basis of the diagnosis; and a means to deal with the lack of motivation and skills on the part of the low achiever. These sensitivities are not to be found in the traditional sense of individualized instruction. They are found, however, in well-designed systems of structured tutoring. The increasing amount of empirical evidence on structured tutoring will support this position.

Based upon the premise that structured tutoring is effective in remediating learning deficiencies, the question surfaces as to the best method of implementing tutorial programs in our schools. Should teachers be used as the tutors? Should volunteer parents? Older students? Or should peer students be used? PEER STUDENTS? Yes, that's right, peer students!

First of all, teachers are too busy and too few to tutor all those who need to be tutored. Parents are great, if you can get enough of them to willingly and consistently *donate* their time and effort. Older students, especially those from other schools, are good, but they are often harder to obtain than willing parents. It follows, then, that since peer tutors come from the same class, grade, or school, the only thing that may prevent their use is that teachers are given no flexibility by the administration to incorporate such a plan. Otherwise, there are almost always sufficient numbers of potential tutors who are more than willing to participate. At this point, let me clarify something in the mind of the reader: *peer tutoring does work!* There is enough evidence, both anecdotal and empirical, which indicates that peer tutorial learning is effective. Sure, there have been some inconclusive studies, but this is true in any area of study. In addition, the great majority of the inconclusive studies did not involve a true *structured tutorial* format. Loosely conceived and implemented tutorial programs will fail more often than not.

If we can now accept the idea that peer tutoring *will work,* if properly organized and implemented, coupled with the easy access teachers have in selecting and utilizing peer tutors, we can now outline some specifics.

Most tutorial situations are visualized as one-to-one interactions. Although it is true that this type of interaction seems to be the most effective, tutorial programs with up to five learners in a tutorial group have been highly successful. The capability of the tutors, the number of tutors available, and the number of learners to be tutored are all important considerations in determining group size. However, in working with slow or disadvantaged learners, or low achievers, the one-to-one interaction is best.

At this point, it should be remembered that regardless of the size of the tutorial group and the structure of the tutorial materials, the organizer should always reserve an area for tutorial activities that is uncrowded and relatively quiet with minimum distraction. It is usually in a distraction-free environment that tutorial instruction demonstrates its natural superiority as an instructional format.

Peer tutorial learning may take place in any group where you have the following:

1. The tutors can *at least* read and (if working in math) have a thorough understanding of simple borrowing and carrying procedures.
2. The tutors and tutees can *both* understand and follow simple directions.
3. The tutors and tutees have an attention span of *at least* 15 minutes.
4. The tutors have no obvious debilitating character- istics—cognitive, affective, or psychomotor—which would prevent accomplishment of the desired task.

As the reader can now appreciate, peer tutorial learning will work at any grade level where the above conditions apply.

An additional important aspect of tutoring is that it can apply to any subject area. Whether the subject is cognitive (understanding), affective (feeling), or psychomotor (muscle movement), peer tutorial learning can be effective and efficient. For example, one can be just as successful in using peers to tutor reading, math, and music as in art, golf, and typing.

The limitations in applying peer tutorial instruction are few, if any. However, the reader should keep the point firmly in mind that there is little instructional advantage in having students tutor other students *unless the instruction is specified and controlled.* Thus, the strength of any tutorial program is in its organizational development and implementa- tion.

It may be surprising to some, but tutorial instruction does not benefit only the tutee (the person being tutored). In fact, one of the most interesting results to emerge from research on tutoring concerns its effects upon the peer *tutor.* Benefits to the peer tutor, besides specific learning improvements, are positive changes in self-concept, motivation, attitude, and social behavior. The amazing thing is that these facilitating effects have been known for years. Joseph Lancaster, in a book published in 1803, stated: ". . . I have ever found, the surest way to cure a mischievous boy was to make him a monitor (tutor). I never knew anything to succeed much better, if as well." Lancaster was not alone in his feeling about peer tutoring, even in the early 1800's. It is thus interesting to speculate as to why peer tutorial instruction in American schools has not received the plaudits it so richly deserves. This is especially true in light of its long known superiority as an instructional system.

There are no *consistent* empirical differences between students being tutored by their peers or tutored from non-peers. There is, however, some evidence which suggests that a greater age difference between tutor and tutee results in slightly better tutee cognitive performance. But, on the other hand, the nature of the interaction may be more pleasant when the age range between tutor and tutee is closer, thus fostering more positive feelings toward learning in general.

As inflation continues to shrink the value of the dollar and as the population stabilizes, not only will greater instructional effectiveness be desired, but also increased instructional efficiency. Through proper conceptualization, structuring, and implementing of peer tutorial systems, both of the above desires may be easily realized.

II.

OPERATIONAL DESCRIPTION

Peer Tutorial Instruction is a process in which students are selected and trained to tutor someone their own age or younger in a specified area of learning. The tutorial group may vary in size; but when working with low achievers, the one-to-one interaction is recommended.

There are two important factors to consider when setting up a peer tutorial system. The first is to realize that if real learning gains are desired, it is going to take a significant effort on the part of the organizer to develop, structure, and implement the system. The old axiom that "one gets out what effort one puts in," or "garbage in, garbage out," applies especially in the development of peer tutorial systems.

The second factor is to understand that if any of the following suggested procedures is omitted, the desired learning gains will likely decrease from what could have occurred. These procedures have been empirically demonstrated to be effective in a wide variety of remediation efforts.

In this chapter, we will briefly look at each of the following steps, stressing their most salient parts. In the "Design Format" chapter, examples and greater elaboration will be made so that the reader can have a much better "feel" for setting up his or her own peer tutoring program.

(1) selecting the learners (tutees);

(2) determining the instructional objectives;

(3) designing diagnostic pretests and outlining pretesting procedures;

(4) developing comprehensive student record forms and record-keeping procedures;

(5) developing and structuring the instructional materials;

(6) designing a Tutor Log and Tutor Assignment Sheet;

(7) determining the tutorial group size;

(8) selecting and training peer tutors;

(9) determining instructional assignments and reviews;

(10) designing a posttest and a Summative Learning Gains Record;

(11) developing a schedule for the peer tutors; and

(12) monitoring the peer tutors and the tutorial system.

Although there are some good complete tutorial systems and partial systems on the market, there are also some poor ones. Rather than completely developing your own system, you may elect to select, from some of the good systems, those parts that may be helpful to you. Regardless of what you select, keep in mind that it should "fit" one or more of the 12 topics in the list above.

1. Selecting the Learners (Tutees)

Out of the 12 topics listed in setting up a peer tutorial system, this one is probably the easiest. Classroom teachers usually know, without much thought, those students in need of remediation. This is true whether it is in reading, math, English, attitudes, or psychomotor skills. This knowledge comes from a variety of sources, ranging from standardized test results, to homework assignments, to teacher-made tests, to classroom performance. If, however, you are selecting students outside your own classroom, it is best to contact individual teachers in selecting your tutees. A note of caution: be sure to emphasize that you don't want only those students with disruptive behavior problems. (That is, unless your peer tutorial program specifically addresses these problems.) The students you want are those with learning deficiencies. Of course, they may be one and the same, but in many cases, disruptive behavior problems don't go hand-in-hand with learning deficiencies.

If the peer tutorial system is going to be an ongoing program, decisions will have to be made as to which students are to be tutored initially. It is recommended that those students experiencing the most serious learning problems, yet who have the basic prerequisite skills necessary for adequate understanding of the learning tasks, be tutored first.

2. Determining the Instructional Objectives
A. *Rationale*

Without written goals and instructional objectives, no tutorial program—peer or otherwise—will come close to reaching its potential; in essence, ending up somewhere other than in success. An additional and most important point is that these *written goals and objectives need to be stated with great specificity.* One of the main reasons why peer tutorial programs often fail is the lack of precision and specificity in the stated instructional objectives and goals. For example, when working with beginning readers, an instructional objective, such as "each student will learn how to read Dr. Seuss' books," is too broad. On the other hand, an objective stating "each child will be able to produce the sounds of all the vowels with no errors or hesitation" is a specific objective. The chances of well-defined learning outcomes are significantly enhanced with specific objectives.

B. *Construction*

There are four important factors to keep in mind when stating your specific instructional objectives.

1. *Be sensitive to the entering behaviors of the students*

to be tutored. Do they have the basic prerequisite skills in order to successfully understand and complete your instructional objectives? If they do, you are right on target. If they don't, then you will either have to revise your objectives or find other students with the appropriate prerequisite skills.

2. *Be aware that peer tutorial systems are not always for remediation purposes only.* Your instructional objectives can be designed to give your average students intellectual challenges, as possible preparation for some future presentation of complex material. You can thus effectively ward off anticipated slowdowns in your instruction. This is especially true in the "hard" sciences.

3. *Objectives should be stated in terms of observable and measurable student performance.* For example, the tutees should actually provide, either vocally or in written form, the correct responses to specific tasks indicated by the instructional materials of the tutor.

4. Since the great majority of peer tutoring involves a stimulus-response type of learning, it is important to stipulate that *the student respond correctly without any hesitation.* Also, if there is a sequence involved in a specific task, the student should be able to provide the correct answers when *the stimuli are presented out of sequence.*

3. Designing Diagnostic Pretests and Outlining Pretesting Procedures

A. *Rationale*

The purpose of most diagnoses is to assess specific situations. These are then usually followed by prescriptions if the diagnoses have revealed problems. Thus, in the construction of your diagnostic pretest, the testing stimuli should begin with simple items or tasks. With this method, you can effectively locate the specific area of difficulty and then "prescribe" the appropriate entry point to your instructional program.

In a peer tutorial instructional program, the supervisor, or even the tutor, if well trained, can specify the instructional entry step for the tutee. Of course, this means that the instructional program is also hierarchically arranged. In other words, the instructional tasks go from simple to those more difficult.

B. *Administering the Pretest*

Before administering the pretest, special consideration should be given to reducing anxiety in the testing situation. The peer tutor and tutee should meet each other and briefly chat about a common interest, i.e., pets, sports, teachers, etc. Friendly communication is a *must* on the part of the peer tutor or test administrator. The following points should then be carefully followed by the administrator when administering the pretest:

1. Read the directions slowly and ask if the tutee understands them. If he or she doesn't, repeat the directions and further clarify, if necessary. Your directions may be too complicated; keep them easy to understand.

2. Point to each stimulus with a pencil and have the student give a response.

3. *DO NOT* give any feedback as to whether the responses are correct or incorrect. But do encourage the tutee with statements like "You're doing fine. Keep doing your best."

4. If the student hesitates *more than one second,* or says "I don't know," mark the response as incorrect and then say to the tutee, "That's okay, let's go on to the next item." (If the student cannot recognize the item within approximately one second, he or she most likely doesn't know the stimulus.)

5. If the student responds correctly within one second, mark the response as correct.

(Note: In marking the response, the pretest administrator should use a predetermined system for distinguishing correct from incorrect items; for example, a circle around the stimulus for a correct response (e.g., (the)) and a circle with a small loop at the top for an incorrect response (e.g., (the)). There is nothing sacred about this system. Keep in mind, however, that the marks used in determining correct from incorrect items should be similar but have one slight difference that is discernible to someone who looks closely. Also, be sure to standardize the marking procedure so that all those administering your pretest use the same system. The reason for marking every response given by the student is to avoid calling special attention to only incorrect items, thus successfully avoiding increased test anxiety.)

6. If your pretest is hierarchically arranged, and if the tutee misses four or five items in a row, terminate the pretest and assign all further anticipated responses as incorrect.

4. Developing Comprehensive Student Record Forms and Record-Keeping Procedures

A. *Rationale*

Without a prescribed form and definite procedures for keeping track of each student's performance, there is little reason to systematize instruction. Student performance records are absolutely necessary in assessing weaknesses from pretest performance and in assessing student progress from interaction with the instructional materials.

If your record-keeping form is well-designed and if the procedures for updating student performance are clear, peer tutors will have no difficulty with this phase in the operational design.

B. *Record-Keeping Procedures*

Following administration of the pretest, the results and present date should be *immediately* posted on the Student Record Form. The same system used in identifying correct from incorrect items on the pretest should be used on the Student Record Form (e.g., ⊙ for correct and ⊗ for incorrect items, or whatever system you decide to use.) However, remember now to *emphasize* the differences between the two marks to eliminate any potential confusion.

In posting the learning stimuli prescriptions, care should be used in recording the correct date of each individual prescription. It should be pointed out that *no more than six prescriptions* to learn in one tutorial session should be given. Often, you will find that some slower tutees will be over-challenged by six prescriptions. In working with the student a short while, the peer tutor will develop a "feel" for how many learning stimuli prescriptions he or she can realistically give in each tutorial session.

Mastery is determined when the tutee can provide the correct response to a learning stimulus three different and separate times without hesitation. The date this happens is recorded by the tutor in the mastery date section under the appropriate stimuli column.

Learning checks are periodically made every two or three weeks to insure accurate retention. The date of each learning check for each stimulus is then properly recorded by the tutor.

Following administration of the posttest, the results and date should also be immediately posted. Comparisons between pretest and posttest performance should now be easy to make.

5. Developing and Structuring the Instructional Materials
A. *Rationale*

The instructional materials are very important to the

overall success of your peer tutorial system. If they are weak, your instructional gains will be greatly reduced from what could be realized if the materials are clear, simple, well-organized, and instructionally strong.

B. *Two Approaches*

There are various approaches one could use in developing, or even purchasing, instructional materials appropriate for tutoring. However, there are two successful approaches worthy of special mention because of their effectiveness. The first involves mimeographed pages with six learning stimuli per page. The peer tutor works with the tutee on a page-by-page basis, teaching each of the stimuli on every page. To insure that the tutee isn't learning the stimuli by sequence cueing alone (learning the order of the stimuli as a separate entity), one or preferably two additional sheets with identical stimuli, but in different order on each page, will work nicely. If the peer tutor will use all three sheets during the tutorial session, learning will be greatly enhanced.

If this method is adopted, it is highly recommended that the instructional stimuli pages have holes punched for use in a two or three ring binder. Each peer tutor should have his or her own binder. These binders could also be used to keep the pretest and Student Record Form for easy access by the peer tutor and supervisor. Of course, they should be in an indexed and separate section of the binder, apart from the instructional materials.

The other, or second, method involves the use of 3x5 flash cards. If possible, it is best to have one set of flash cards per peer tutor, with three flash cards of each learning stimulus. Also, each tutor should be provided with a file box or shoe box with index cards in which to store and organize the complete set of flash cards. Flash card usage will be discussed in detail in the "Design Format" chapter.

6. Designing a Tutor Log and Tutor Assignment Sheet
A. *Rationale*

A Tutor Log, which contains the instructional activity of each peer tutor, is a necessity in any tutorial system. First, it provides a complete record of the learning progress accomplished by the peer tutor and tutee. Second, it assists the supervisor in keeping track of how frequently the peer tutor has worked with the tutee. Third, it helps to clarify the problems encountered in the tutorial sessions.

When you have peer tutors working with more than one tutee, it is logistically wise to inform the tutors of pertinent information regarding each tutee. This can be done with what is called a Tutor Assignment Sheet. This form is easy to develop and can be used in whatever way is most helpful to the supervisor in coordinating tutorial activities.

B. *Two Log Formats*

There are two effective log formats, incorporating the above items, that you might consider. The first is designed primarily for those young peer tutors whose writing skills are limited. It involves short activity statements, with a box to check if the activity is accomplished. Similar short progress statements, with the accompanying check boxes, are also in the log. Thus, all the young tutor has to do is to check the appropriate boxes, rather than make poor attempts at writing down an involved description of the activities and progress made during the tutorial session.

You may have already guessed the second log format from the above description. Instead of having short statements with check boxes, an adequate space should be provided for peer tutor comments under the tutorial activity column and the progress column.

C. *The Tutor Assignment Sheet*

The Tutor Assignment Sheet should include pertinent instructions you think would be well for the tutor to have. But, mostly, the Tutor Assignment Sheet is designed to inform the classroom teacher and tutor who he or she will be tutoring, what time to begin tutoring, where to tutor, and what to tutor.

7. Determining the Tutorial Group Size

The most effective group size in tutorial instruction, which has been mentioned earlier, is the one-to-one interaction. By all means, if you are just starting a peer tutorial program, begin with one-to-one interactions only. As your tutors become more experienced and sophisticated, you may elect to try assigning two or more tutees per tutor.

Don't be afraid to experiment in seeking greater instructional effectiveness and efficiency. However, whether you experiment with the tutorial materials, record forms, tests, group size, etc., keep foremost in mind that it is quite improper and unethical to sacrifice someone's learning progress for experimental purposes only.

8. Selecting and Training Peer Tutors

A. *Selection*

In the selection of tutors, beyond their possessing the basic prerequisite skills outlined in the "Use" chapter, three personality characteristics are desirable. *Dependability* is the most important of the three. Select those peer tutors you can consistently count on to be present when their tutorial session begins. The other two characteristics are *understanding* and *patience.* These two are often called upon when a tutee is emotionally upset or is experiencing only marginal success.

Some additional helpful thoughts are that the tutors selected should be well thought of by their peers. Also, an even number of tutors is desirable, since there is a lot of one-to-one practice during training sessions. When first starting your program, it is advisable to select ten or 12 peer tutors as a maximum. Any more tutors presents problems for the supervisor during the training sessions. These training problems will be discussed further in the section on training.

The tutor's academic ability in many tutorial systems is not a critical factor. However, it *is* in peer tutorial systems. When using tutors to teach their peers, intellectual differences are much closer than if an adult were tutoring a child. Thus, it can be intimidating and counterproductive when the tutee ends up explaining directions and even correcting the tutor during the tutorial session.

In some instances, peer tutorial systems have been successful at the third grade level, although those particular third graders were intellectually brighter than most. More success has been obtained with fourth grade peer tutors, and even more has been accomplished with fifth and sixth grade peer tutors. *Generally speaking,* fifth and sixth graders make the best elementary tutors.

There has been some attempt to gather data on whether females are better tutors than males; however, no consistent superiority has been found for either sex. In any event, selecting the mix of boys and girls is strictly up to the discretion of the supervisor.

B. *Training*

The success of your tutorial program depends not only on how well the peer tutors have been selected, but also on how well they have been trained. The actual training should consist of three or four 50-minute sessions. It is imperative that every tutor attend all of the training sessions. A word or two, such as that those not attending all of the sessions will be dropped from the program, is often the only motivation you will have to provide. Keep in mind that being selected and trained as a tutor has real prestige. To lose that prestige is not a desirable thing; thus, most young tutors who are selected will work hard.

The size of the training sessions should be limited to *ten or 12 tutors* at most. Since they will be working in pairs during the practice part of the session, most supervisors will be hard-pressed to observe, supervise, and make corrections with five or six pairs of tutors.

The specific areas in which all tutors need to be thoroughly trained consist of the following:

(1) introductory techniques;

(2) general tutoring procedures;

(3) pretesting and posttesting procedures;

(4) properly filling out the Student Record Forms;

(5) tutoring from the instructional materials;

(6) properly filling out the Tutor Log;

(7) determining the instructional assignments and reviews; and

(8) properly filling out the Summative Learning Gains Record.

Before leaving this section, an important point needs to be stressed. During the training sessions for each of the eight items, the trainer needs to first *explain* the procedure or technique, then *demonstrate* it, and then require each tutor to *practice* it with his or her role-playing partner tutor. The trainer supervises all practice, insuring that all tutors are proficient in each task before going on to the next. If this procedure is followed closely, each tutor will be well trained and ready for the "real" tutoring.

9. Determining Instructional Assignments and Reviews

Making instructional assignments is a simple task, especially if pretesting procedures went well and the results were accurately posted on the Student Record Forms. From these results, the instructional assignments are given, consisting of those stimuli missed on the pretest. However, if your pretest was designed with generalization to additional stimuli in mind, then those additional stimuli would form the instructional assignments.

Remember that in dealing with youngsters, it is best to

limit the number of new stimuli to learn, per tutorial session, to six items. You may elect to have only four or five stimuli to learn in the first session, then go to six in the following sessions.

If older students are involved, such as junior high or high school students, more stimuli per session may be advisable. The supervisor will have to use judgment as to what is best for the tutors and tutees involved.

Once the initial stimuli are prescribed, proper notations, such as the date for each stimulus, are posted on the Student Record Form. Once mastery has been obtained, e.g., *the student recalling each stimulus in three separate sessions with no hesitation,* the dates should be posted.

An essential part of any intensive instructional program is review. You will notice, in looking at the Student Record Form in the "Design Format" chapter, that there is space for three separate reviews. A rule-of-thumb in scheduling reviews is that the first review should come approximately *one or two weeks following mastery.* The second review should come *two to three weeks from the first review,* and the third review should come *three to four weeks after the second review.* Remember that this is just a rule-of-thumb and not the only way to schedule reviews. In fact, the supervisor is best qualified to know when reviews should be conducted, and he or she may wish to exceed the time periods suggested.

10. Designing a Posttest and a Summative Learning Gains Record

Rationale

Certainly, anyone interested in demonstrable learning improvement is familiar with why we have posttests. Posttesting is an important part of any peer tutorial system. It is *the* method in which we determine if there has been any empirical learning improvement; and, if there has been such achievement, it determines just *how much.*

An extremely important point to remember about post-testing is that if you desire to have posttest results that will stand close scrutiny, have your tutors exchange students when posttesting. This way, posttesting can be more objective and less emotional. It will, in turn, greatly reduce the chance of tutors intentionally inflating student scores and/or cueing students on specific responses. An additional point is that each student should be introduced, at least a few days before posttesting, to the one who will posttest him or her. This will help to reduce anxiety during testing. Also, tutors should convey to the testers any idiosyncracies of their students which may prevent proper posttest performance.

A useful form to which you will be introduced is the Summative Learning Gains Record. This Record is designed to provide an instant analysis of the performance differential between pretest and posttest. It provides the supervisor with a graphic illustration of not only how well specific tutees improved, but also of how well the overall tutorial program succeeded in meeting its stated objectives.

The Summative Learning Gains Record can be filled out by the tutors or the supervisor. Regardless of the amount of time spent in tutoring, even if it is only two or three sessions, each student terminating the program should be posttested and the Summative Learning Gains Record filled out from the pretest and posttest results. (Student gains are determined by subtracting, for each stimuli group, the pretest score from the posttest score.) This gives the supervisor a complete record of exactly what progress was made and which peer tutor and student made it.

11. Developing a Schedule for the Peer Tutors

In developing any kind of schedule, it is best to first confer with the teachers of the tutors and tutees. They should help you set up specific times so as to minimize distracting other students when the tutors and tutees leave class and later return.

It may be that the location available will dictate not only where, but also when you can meet. The importance of selecting a relatively quiet and distraction-free location was noted above. If this is not readily available, use your imagination in locating a suitable place. You may find yourself in the gym, the school kitchen, or even hallways. Whatever the place, make the best of it.

When working with other teachers, above all be courteous, gentle, persuasive, and honest. Let them help you set up the schedule; don't dictate to them. If problems arise in the schedule, react to them immediately. Don't let potential problems get started or upset your plans. Keep teachers up-to-date in schedule changes. Each teacher should be given a list of which students you are working with and in what capacity they are working, i.e., tutor or tutee.

Ideally, peer tutors should work with their tutees on a daily basis, excluding weekends and holidays. If you can arrange for this, great. If not, keep in mind that for your program to be truly effective, *the tutees should be tutored at least three times per week, with at least 15 to 20 minutes per session.* Keep these figures as a bargaining point with those teachers and administrators who might try to give you a difficult time in either scheduling or implementing your program.

12. Monitoring the Peer Tutors
and the Tutorial System
A. *The Tutors*

One of the major reasons for tutorial program failure is that the tutors involved begin to deviate from the prescribed instructional procedures. Thus, the program becomes a messy "hodge-podge" of several programs. If you, as the organizer and developer, want success, then carefully design your peer tutorial program and then insure that the design is followed. If you do experience failure, at least you will know that it was the fault of the design. Thus, you can change the design to insure success. However, if every tutor is doing his or her own thing and then you experience failure, you would have no way of knowing whether it was the tutors who failed or if your design was faulty.

A successful method for insuring that your peer tutors follow the specified procedures is to state that those observed not following the procedures will be dropped from the program. Rather than leaving it at this, however, positive reinforcement should be given often to your tutors. Don't hesitate to use praise and encouragement for work well done. A "Tutor of the Week" may be selected to give extra attention to good work.

Some additional important points to consider in monitoring your tutors are:

1. Require your tutors and tutees to be punctual in attending the tutorial session and in returning to class. Teachers who find their students, whether they be tutors or tutees, walking in the halls or late in returning to class will take a dim view of releasing future students for the program.

2. Exchange those peer tutors who experience personality problems with their tutees. Be aware of these potential problems when assigning the peer tutors.

3. Some tutors may become disinterested after a while and want to leave the program. Talk with them and carefully observe if there is a specific reason for their disinterest. If there is, it may be easy to remedy. If it cannot be resolved, then don't force students to continue tutoring if they don't want to do so. However, if care has been taken in all the areas of development and implementation, most peer tutors will continue to work effectively.

B. *The Tutorial System*

In monitoring a peer tutorial program, care should be

exercised to be as objective as possible. Even though it is "your baby," be open to critical suggestions.

Probably the most important aspect in monitoring your program is to check from time to time to see if your stated objectives are being successfully met. If they are not, then you may have to alter either your objectives or the program—most likely, the latter. An additional point to consider is to carefully monitor the learning review checks. It is in these simple checks that retention of learned stimuli is reinforced, thus permitting better posttest scores on the part of the tutees.

Since you will be the designer of your own peer tutorial program, keep the records of your successes and failures, both in the development and implementation stages. These records can be valuable when making changes and in reporting results.

III.

DESIGN FORMAT

This chapter provides the reader with specific examples, illustrations, and further elaboration of items presented in the "Operational Description" chapter. Thus, each of the 12 steps in implementing a peer tutorial program will be presented, with new emphasis, particularly in light of specific examples and forms needed. Several illustrative samples will be given for each step, thus illustrating the wide range of subjects and levels of instruction possible in utilizing peer tutoring.

1. Selecting the Learners (Tutees)

There is not much one can add in the way of examples and illustrations in selecting learners. Selecting learners is a rather uncomplicated task and is adequately discussed in the "Operational Description" chapter.

2. Determining the Instructional Objectives

Your instructional objectives establish the nature of your tutorial program. Considerable care should be given to the construction of these objectives.

There are many different types of objectives. The following five categories (*A* through *E*) cover fairly broad areas of human behavior. The majority of the sample objectives are from the cognitive domain. Don't be afraid, though, to take on the affective domain if that is your area of concern. It should be remembered, however, that affective objectives are usually more difficult to write and even more difficult to evaluate.

A. Stimulus-Response Objectives

(Social Studies)

1. The student will be able to identify all the Presidents of the United States when given only a picture of each.

    Example:

Stimulus	*The Desired Response*
A picture of Abraham Lincoln	"Abraham Lincoln"

2. The student will be able to identify each state on a map of the United States which has all the state names omitted.

    Example:

Stimulus	*The Desired Response*
	"California"

3. The student will be able to identify all the major wars when presented with a list of the year each war commenced.

    Example:

Stimulus	*The Desired Response*
1941	"World War II"

4. The student will be able to identify, from a large list, the major accomplishment of several world leaders, both in the past and presently.

Example:

Stimulus	The Desired Response
Anwar Sadat	"The Egyptian leader who traveled to Israel to attempt a peace agreement."

(Reading)

1. The student will be able to unhesitatingly produce the sounds of all the consonants.

   Example:

Stimulus	The Desired Response
z	"zzzzzzzz"

2. The student will be able to unhesitatingly produce the short sound of all five vowels.

   Example:

Stimulus	The Desired Response
e	"eh"

3. The student will be able to unhesitatingly produce the sounds of the following digraphs: th, sh, wh, sw, qu, and ng.

   Example:

Stimulus	The Desired Response
th	"th"

4. The student will be able to unhesitatingly produce the sounds of the following blends: bl, fl, gl, sl, br, cr, dr, gr, fr, and pr.

   Example:

Stimulus	The Desired Response
bl	"bl"

5. The student will be able to unhesitatingly read all of the sight words from the list on the next page.

Example:

Stimulus	The Desired Response
about	"about"

Basic Sight Vocabulary

a	done	if	over	think
about	don't	in	own	this
after	down	into	pick	those
again	draw	is	play	three
all	drink	its	please	to
an	eat	jump	pretty	today
am	eight	just	pull	together
always	every	keep	put	too
and	fall	kind	ran	try
any	far	know	read	two
are	fast	laugh	red	under
around	find	let	right	up
as	first	light	round	us
ask	five	like	run	upon
at	fly	little	ride	use
ate	for	long	said	very
be	four	look	say	want
because	from	made	see	warm
been	full	make	seven	was
before	funny	many	she	wash
best	gave	her	shall	we
better	get	may	show	well
big	give	me	sing	went
black	go	much	sit	were
blue	goes	must	six	what
both	going	my	sleep	when
bring	good	myself	small	where
brown	got	never	so	which
but	green	new	some	white
buy	grow	no	soon	who
by	had	now	start	why
call	has	not	stop	will
came	have	of	take	wish
can	he	off	tell	with
carry	help	old	too	work
clean	here	on	thank	would
cold	him	once	that	yellow

come	his	one	the	write
could	hold	only	their	yes
cut	hot	open	them	you
did	how	or	then	your
does	hurt	our	there	yours
do	I	out	these	ours
			they	

(Grammar and Spelling)

1. The student will be able to correctly identify, from a list of sentences, all the parts of speech in each sentence.

Example:

Stimulus	*The Desired Response*
The man went home.	The-"Adjective"
	man-"Noun and Subject"
	went-"Verb"
	home-"Direct Object"

2. The student will be able to unhesitatingly produce, from a list of irregular verbs, the correct past tense of each verb.

Example:

Stimulus	*The Desired Response*
begin	"began"

3. The student will be able to unhesitatingly produce, from an unpunctuated paragraph, all the correct punctuation.

Example:

Stimulus	*The Desired Response*
Each person except Fred went home everyone was happy	"Each person, except Fred, went home. Everyone was happy."

4. The student will be able to unhesitatingly produce, from a list of Spanish words, the English equivalent.

Example:

Stimulus	*The Desired Response*
agua	"water"
libro	"book"

5. The student will be able to unhesitatingly spell, from a list of words, each word correctly.

Example:

| *Stimulus* | *The Desired Response* |
| accommodate | "a-c-c-o-m-m-o-d-a-t-e" |

(Mathematics)

1. The student will be able to unhesitatingly produce the correct answer for each of the following addition facts, when they are randomly presented: $1 + 2 =, 3 + 2 =, 2 + 4 =, 5 + 3 =, 0 + 6 =, 6 + 4 =, 1 + 7 =, 8 + 4 =, 4 + 9 =, 7 + 9 =, 3 + 8 =$.

Example:

| *Stimulus* | *The Desired Response* |
| $5 + 3 =$ | "eight" |

2. The student will be able to unhesitatingly produce the correct answer for each of the following subtraction facts, when they are randomly presented: $3 - 2 =, 5 - 1 =, 7 - 5 =, 8 - 4 =, 12 - 6 =, 13 - 4 =, 11 - 8 =, 14 - 7 =$.

Example:

| *Stimulus* | *The Desired Response* |
| $12 - 6 =$ | "six" |

3. The student will be able to unhesitatingly and correctly read the following numbers: 111, 3,578, 536, 4,659, 0,239, 7,235, 9,377, 10,491.

Example:

| *Stimulus* | *The Desired Response* |
| 3,578 | "three thousand five hundred and seventy eight" |

4. The student will be able to unhesitatingly say how many halves in a whole, how many fourths in a half, how many thirds in a whole, how many sixths in a third, how many eighths in a fourth, etc.

Example:

Stimulus	The Desired Response
1 half = ___ fourths	"two"

5. The student will be able to unhesitatingly say how many grams in a kilogram, how many pints in a gallon, how many pints in a litre, how many cups in a litre, how many inches in a yard, how many inches in a meter, how many grams in an ounce, etc.

Example:

Stimulus	The Desired Response
1 litre = ___ cups	"four point seventeen"

B. Computation Objectives

1. The student will correctly use the borrowing process from the tens and hundreds columns when working subtraction problems.

Example:

Problem	The Desired Response
725	725
-358	-358
	367

2. The student will correctly solve long-division problems where there is a remainder.

Example:

Problem

$$22\overline{)8,956}$$

The Desired Response

$$407 \ 2/22$$

$$
\begin{array}{r}
22\overline{)8,956} \\
88 \\
\hline
15 \\
00 \\
\hline
156 \\
154 \\
\hline
2
\end{array}
$$

3. The student will correctly compute the value of x when given ten problems of the following type: $3x + 8 = 26$.

Example:

Problem	*The Desired Response*
$6x + 20 = 140$	$6x = 140 - 20$
	$6x = 120$ $\qquad$ $x = 20$
	$x = \dfrac{120}{6}$

4. The student will correctly compute the interest paid in ten problems dealing with simple interest.

Example:

Problem	*The Desired Response*
Bill is paying 18% interest on a one year loan of $5,000. How much interest will he pay?	5000
	.18
	40000
	50000
	$900.00

C. Time, Measurement, and Calculation

1. The student will be able to point on a clock that has no hands, the correct position the clock hands should be in, when given verbally several different times.

Example:

Stimulus	*The Desired Response*
10:30	"The large hand will be on the six and the short hand will be on the ten."

2. The student will be able to correctly measure in inches and centimeters the length of several objects provided by the teacher.

Example:

Stimulus	*The Desired Response*
The height of a typical door.	"Eighty four inches or two hundred and twelve and sixteen one hundredths centimeters."

3. The student will be able to correctly compute problems dealing with the time it takes to travel specified distances when given the rate of speed. (R x T = D)

Example:

Stimulus	*The Desired Response*
When Ted left home, it was six o'clock. He traveled at a rate of 60 m.p.h. How long did it take to arrive at his destination, if he traveled for 500 miles?	"Eight hours and 20 minutes."

4. The student will be able to give an accurate combination of different monies which will sum up to the following figures: $7.39, $8.52, $15.94, $37.65, $73.16, $104.37, $250.42.

Example:

Stimulus	*The Desired Response*
$8.52	"One five dollar bill, three one dollar bills, one fifty cent piece (or five dimes, or ten nickles), and two pennies."

D. Rule Application

1. The student will be able to write the correct plural noun form for several provided nouns, according to the rules for that type of noun.

Example:

Stimulus	*The Desired Response*
honey	"honeys"

2. The student will be able to correctly capitalize all words in a long paragraph that fit the rules for capitalization of countries, states, cities, and religions.

Example:

Stimulus	*The Desired Response*
southern arizona is much influenced by its neighbor to the south, mexico. phoenix is arizona's capital city and there are many mexican-american catholics that live there.	"Southern Arizona is much influenced by its neighbor to the south, Mexico. Phoenix is Arizona's capital city and there are many Mexican-American Catholics that live there."

3. The student will be able to correctly conjugate, in French, unfamiliar regular verbs which end in "ir."

Example:

Stimulus	*The Desired Response*
finir	"je finis, nous finissons, tu finis, vous finissez, il finit, ils finissent."

4. The student will be able to correctly spell the following words containing "ie" and "ei" combinations, and be able to state the spelling rule for each word: believe, brief, chief, leisure, receive, seize.

Example:

Stimulus	*The Desired Response*
receive	"r-e-c-e-i-v-e. Because the letter 'c' comes before the letter combination, 'ei' must be used."

E. Psychomotor

1. The student will be able to legibly write, in longhand, ten examples of all the letters of the alphabet.

Example:

Stimulus	*The Desired Response*
a	"a a a a a a a a a a"
b	"b b b b b b b b b b"

2. The student will be able to draw examples of squares, triangles, circles, rectangles, cylinders, and octagons, so that the lines are all connected and not over-drawn.

Example:

Stimulus

The Desired Response
" "

3. The student will be able to bounce a basketball 15 times with each hand without having to stop at any time.

Example:

Stimulus	*The Desired Response*
given a basketball	"Right hand, bounce, bounce, bounce . . . left hand, bounce, bounce, bounce . . ."

4. The student will be able to putt a golf ball into a regulation golf hole with a regulation putter from five feet out, eight out of ten times.

Example:

Stimulus	*The Desired Response*
Given a regulation putter on a regulation golf green.	"Putt the ball in the hole at least eight out of ten times."

3. Designing Diagnostic Pretests and Outlining Pretesting Procedures

In the "Operational Description" chapter, specific procedural steps were outlined for administering a diagnostic pretest. In this chapter, two specific examples will be given, illustrating the design and administration procedures of a pretest in reading and in math. See Figures 1 and 2.

Regardless of the pretest's subject matter, there are a few specific items which should be on all pretests. These are:

(1) a place to record the student's name, age, grade, school, and teacher;

(2) a place to record the date the pretest was administered;

(3) a place to record the name of the person who administered the pretest;

(4) specific instructions for the test administrator to read to the student; and

(5) the testing stimuli should be hierarchically arranged (advancing from simple to complex).

(Text Continued on Page 49)

Figure 1

A. Pretest in Reading

Pretest Coversheet

Name ....

Age and Grade ....

School and Teacher ....

Date ....

Examiner ....

Comments:

(Continued on Next Page)

Figure 1 (Continued)

Reading Pretest

Peer Tutor Directions

It is important that you relax the tutee following your introduction. Take a few brief minutes to talk about some common interests, i.e., pets, games, friends, etc. Once you feel that he or she is somewhat relaxed, tell him or her you are going to be working with the names and sounds of different letters and words. Tell him or her to do the best he or she can, but if he or she doesn't know the answer, or he or she hesitates longer than *one full second,* say something like: "Don't worry if you don't know it. Let's try the next one and see if we can get it."

Remember that following the tutee's response, mark the stimulus using your previously decided upon technique. For instance, if the tutee responded incorrectly or hesitated too long, mark ⓔ̸ , or if the student responded correctly, mark ⓔ .

Make sure that someone other than yourself can easily recognize your incorrect marks from your correct ones.

When working in the decoding section, Part IV, allow the tutee a couple of attempts to decode the word. If he or she is still struggling after the second attempt or takes *longer than three seconds,* mark it incorrect and go on to the next word. If the student misses *at least three in a row* and seems to be struggling a lot, terminate the test and mark the rest of the words as incorrect. Again, use the same incorrect and correct marks in this part of the pretest as you have in other parts. Note: If the student isn't clear as to what to do, demonstrate or give one example of how the tutee should respond. Also, remember to give no feedback to the tutee as to whether his or her responses are right or wrong, because you are testing, not instructing.

Part I: The Names of the Letters

(Peer Tutor Reads to Tutee): "When I point to each one of these letters, I want you to tell me the name of the letter. If you don't know it or can't remember it, just say, 'I don't know it' or 'I can't remember,' and we will go on to the next letter, okay?"

(Continued on Next Page)

Figure 1 (Continued)

x	s	m	l	r
i	t	p	c	g
b	e	h	w	j
o	y	k	d	v
z	u	n	a	f

Part II: The Sounds of the Letters

(Peer Tutor Reads to Tutee): "When I point to each of these vowels, tell me the *short sound* of that vowel. If you don't know the vowel sound, say 'I don't know,' and we will go on to the next one. Don't worry if you don't know these sounds, okay?"

a	e	i	o	u

(Peer Tutor Reads to Tutee): "When I point to each of these consonants, tell me the sound of that consonant. If you don't know the correct sound, say 'I don't know,' and we will go on to the next one. Don't worry if you don't know all these sounds, okay?"

r	g	j	v	f
l	c	w	d	n
m	p	h	k	z
s	t	y	b	x

(Peer Tutor Reads to Tutee): "When I point to each of these digraphs, or two letter combinations, tell me the sound that they make. If you don't know the correct sound, say 'I don't know,' and we will go on to the next one. Don't worry if you don't know all the sounds, okay?"

(Continued on Next Page)

Figure 1 (Continued)

sh	ng	nk	th	qu	ck	wh	ch

Part III: Basic Sight Words

(Peer Tutor Reads to Tutee): "When I point to each of these words, *read the word out loud*. If you don't know the word, say 'I don't know,' and we will go on to the next one. Don't worry if there are some words you cannot read, okay?"

I	is	are	see	to
is	on	my	this	the
said	that	was	where	there
were	they	he	have	you
		could		

Part IV: Decoding

(Peer Tutor Reads to Tutee): "When I point to each of these words, I want you to read the word out loud. These words are not real and they may sound funny, but I still want you to try to read them as best you can. Again, don't worry if there are some words you can't read. If you can't read a particular word, just say, 'I can't read that one,' and we will go on to the next word, okay?"

ven	yob	zir	luf	jit
rov	kum	sab	deg	bax

sath	whang	sham	zick	quid
chun	shink	banth	thub	brnk

(Continued on Next Page)

Figure 1 (Continued)

twest	prash	blonk	shemp
strim	relib	mring	strish

cremon	bralfib	dremquib
monglinging	chelsam	klingribed
flodmills	thamrant	plarstull

Figure 2

B. Pretest in Mathematics

Pretest Coversheet

Name ....

Age and Grade ....

School and Teacher ....

Date ....

Examiner ....

Comments:

(Continued on Next Page)

Figure 2 (Continued)

Mathematics Pretest

Peer Tutor Directions

It is important that you relax your student after you have made your introductions. Talk to each other a few minutes in order to reduce the test anxiety the student may have. Once you feel he or she is not tense, inform the student he or she is going to be working with some math problems. Also state that there may be some problems he or she cannot work. When the student can't work a particular problem, tell him or her, "Don't worry about solving this problem, let's go on to the next one and try to work it." You should, however, emphasize that the most important thing for the student is for him or her to try to correctly work as many problems as he or she can.

Remember to mark the student's solution as either correct or incorrect, using the method decided upon by your supervisor. For instance, if the student correctly solved $2 + 4 = $ ⑥, then circle the answer. If the student incorrectly solved $2 + 4 = $ ⑧, then circle the answer and include a small loop at the tip of the circle.

For more difficult problems, involving borrowing and carrying, give a little more time for the proper solutions. As for the very simple math fact problems, allow about *two seconds* for the student to give the proper answer. If he or she takes longer, mark the problem as incorrect, then go on to the next problem.

If the student misses three or four problems in a row, then terminate the test and mark the remaining problems as incorrect. Note: If the student isn't clear as to what to do, demonstrate or give the solution for one example so he or she has the task well in mind. Also, remember to give no feedback to the student as to whether his or her responses are right or wrong because you are testing, not instructing.

Part I: The Names of the Numbers

(Peer Tutor Reads to Tutee): "When I point to each one of these numbers, I want you to tell me the *name* of the number. If you don't know it or can't remember it, just say 'I don't know it,' or 'I can't remember,' and we will go on to the next number, okay?"

(Continued on Next Page)

Figure 2 (Continued)

4	2	9
0	3	7
1	8	6
5	10	

(Peer Tutor Reads to Tutee): "When I point to each of these larger numbers, *tell me the number.* If you don't know it, just say 'I don't know it,' and we will go on to the next number, okay?"

35	72	374	1,649
4,927	780	41	13
99	8,333	2,009	454
5,800	63	159	901
3,431	616	50	6,611
877	19	7,123	202
4,987	314	45	9,050

Part II: Addition Math Facts

(Peer Tutor Reads to Tutee): "Now we are going to be working with some addition math fact problems. When I point to a problem, give me the answer to that problem. If you don't know it, just say 'I don't know that one,' and we will go on to the next problem, okay?"

4 + 8 = ____	1 + 3 = ____	2 + 9 = ____	7 + 0 = ____
6 + 7 = ____	5 + 4 = ____	3 + 2 = ____	9 + 1 = ____

(Continued on Next Page)

Figure 2 (Continued)

5	4	9	0
+1	+8	+3	+8
7	2	6	9
+4	+2	+8	+8

10 + 5 =____ 14 + 3 =____ 7 + 12 =____ 8 + 11 =____
11 + 10 =____ 16 + 13 =____ 12 + 14 =____ 15 + 17 =____

5	3	14	13
+11	+12	+ 4	+ 5
12	13	16	11
+17	+14	+10	+18

Part III: Subtraction Math Facts

(Peer Tutor Reads to Tutee): "Now we are going to be working with some subtraction math fact problems. When I point to a problem, give me the answer to that problem. If you don't know it, just say 'I don't know that one,' and we will go on to the next problem, okay?"

8 - 4 =____ 2 - 0 =____ 7 - 3 =____ 9 - 7 =____
6 - 3 =____ 4 - 2 =____ 8 - 7 =____ 5 - 3 =____

9	7	5	6
-4	-3	-0	-2
8	4	9	7
-3	-1	-6	-6

(Continued on Next Page)

Figure 2 (Continued)

| 13 - 6 =____ | 17 - 3 =____ | 11 - 7 =____ | 19 - 8 =____ |
| 14 - 10 =____ | 16 - 12 =____ | 18 - 11 =____ | 17 - 13 =____ |

13	15	12	14
- 7	- 9	- 5	- 8
17	15	19	16
-11	-14	-12	-13

Part IV: Addition Problems Involving Carrying

(Peer Tutor Reads to Tutee): "We are now going to work with some addition problems involving carrying. When I point to a problem, work out the answer for that problem. If you can't work it, just say 'I don't know how to work it,' and we will go on to the next problem, okay?"

27	46	63	39	82
+35	+44	+28	+58	+19
56	76	83	95	63
+47	+65	+48	+39	+57

156	539	482	325
+274	+374	+438	+177
584	697	738	858
+836	+456	+574	+698

| 1,853 | 6,475 | 5,483 |
| +3,594 | +4,736 | +8,689 |

(Continued on Next Page)

Figure 2 (Continued)

Part V: Subtraction Problems Involving Borrowing

(Peer Tutor Reads to Tutee): "We are now going to work with some subtraction problems involving borrowing. When I point to a problem, work out the answer for that problem. If you can't work it, just say 'I don't know how to work it,' and we will go on to the next problem, okay?"

55	63	78	81	94
-27	-44	-39	-45	-66
42	73	60	21	85
-27	-59	-41	-16	-37

274	547	953	716
-166	-228	-538	-409
468	742	631	885
-289	-456	-297	-386

5,376	7,531	8,411
-2,887	-5,956	-3,647

4. Developing Comprehensive Student Record Forms and Record-Keeping Procedures

There are two types of Student Record Forms which will usually meet the needs of even the most rigorous peer tutorial programs. The first type (see Figure 3) is designed for stimulus-response tasks. The second (see Figure 4) is designed mostly for computation, measurement, and rule application tasks.

A note should be added that the second example is quite open-ended and takes a little more expertise on the part of the tutor to fill out. Also, the examples on a computation, measurement, or rule application type of pretest give more of an indication of *general* learning deficiencies or strengths, whereas the stimulus-response type identifies very specific deficiencies or strengths.

These forms, or other forms of your own design, should be filled out on each student immediately following pretesting and posttesting. They should also be continuously updated following each tutorial session so that a complete up-to-date performance record of every student is made.

Student Record Form Construction

A good Student Record Form will have all of the following items:

  (1) a place to record the student's name, age, grade, school, and teacher;
  (2) a brief description of the learning task;
  (3) the specific stimuli as stipulated by the instructional objectives;
  (4) a place to record the date the pretest was administered and a separate place to record the student's performance on the pretest;
  (5) a place to record the specific learning stimuli prescriptions and the date the prescriptions were made;
  (6) a place to record the date mastery was achieved for each stimulus; and

Figure 3

Student Record Form
(Stimulus-Response Example)

Name .... Age .... Grade .... School ...., Teacher ....

Task	(Write a brief description of the learning task.)
Stimuli	(List in these boxes those stimulus items obtained from the pretest and all other, yet similar, stimuli you feel are appropriate. Use additional sheets, if necessary.)
Pretest Date:	(Write the pretest date on the line, then list under each stimulus those items which were indicated as correct or incorrect on the pretest. Use your same system for correct and incorrect items, or use O 's and ⚬ 's, or X's and O's, or +'s and -'s.)
Prescription Date	(List under each stimulus the date that instruction began for that stimulus.)
Mastery Date	(List the date that each stimulus was mastered.)
Review Check — Date / O or ⚬	(List the date of the review for each stimulus and the result of the student's response, correct or incorrect.)
Review Check — Date / O or ⚬	
Review Check — Date / O or ⚬	
Posttest Date:	(Write the posttest date on the line, then list under each stimulus those items which were indicated as correct or incorrect on the posttest. Again, use the same system you used on the pretest and review checks.)

Figure 4

Student Record Form
(Computation, Measurement, and Rule Application Example)

Name ...., Age ...., Grade ...., School ...., Teacher ....

Pretest Date ...., Objective .... Each student will be able to calculate long division problems with an uneven remainder. ....

Date Instruction Began for Each Task	Specific Task to Be Mastered	Mastery Date of Task	Review Check	Posttest Date and Mastery	Comments
Example:					
07/15/78	Dividing thousands into millions and correctly solving nine out of ten problems.	07/30/78	08/15/78	08/30/78 0* *0 = yes X = no	Student experienced little difficulty in learning and remembering the correct rules for solving these long division problems.

(7) a place to record the date for three learning checks and a separate place to record the student's performance on the posttest.

5. Developing and Structuring the Instructional Materials

In the "Operational Description" chapter, it was mentioned that there are two recommended approaches to the development or purchase of successful instructional materials. The first is the mimeographed approach, and the second is the flash card approach.

The mimeod page approach is usually better for the open-ended tasks of computation, measurement, and rule application. On the other hand, the flash card technique is probably the best for stimulus-response tasks. However, remember that both procedures can be successfully used in either type of task.

Two examples of each procedure (see Figures 5-6 and 7-8) will be given on the following pages, plus a description of the techniques used to successfully implement the approaches.

(Text Continued on Page 62)

Figure 5

Mimeographed Sheet Example 1
(Stimulus-Response)

(*Note:* When pretested, the student incorrectly responded to different items. You should print these items on the mimeo sheet. If it is impossible for you to do this with all your students, have the tutors write the incorrect stimulus items on a blank sheet of paper for each of ·their students to use during the tutorial session.)

Sight Words

(Tutor Instructions)
1. Point to one of the sight words and ask your student, "Can you tell me what this word says?" If he or she can't, then say: "This word is 'think.' It is a sight word and can't be correctly sounded out. Can you look at the word and say 'think'?" When the student does so, praise him or her, *then repeat the same process one time,* and go on to the second word.
2. After learning the second sight word, go back and point to the first word and ask, "Can you remember this sight word we learned just a few minutes ago?" If he or she can't, repeat step number 1. If he or she can, praise him or her and then go on to the second sight word on which you have just tutored him or her.
3. Following the student's learning the third sight word, go back and review each of the previous sight words. This review procedure holds for all other words that follow. The student is chaining the words together.
4. In order for the student to better remember each word separately rather than remembering the words only in the context of a sequence, alter the previous sequence, i.e., change the words around. Review each word as often as possible so that as soon as you point to a word, the student correctly responds.
5. To encourage and better motivate the student, have a race or see who can say the word first. Remember to beat him or her a few times to keep him or her competitive. If he or she wins all the time, he or she will soon lose interest.
6. As the student's ability to learn more stimuli increases, you can

(Continued on Next Page)

Figure 5 (Continued)

carefully add more stimuli than the six per session recommended at
the beginning.
7. Remember to consistently praise the student for correct responses.
   Avoid the use of "no" or "that's wrong." Simply demonstrate the
   correct response, if the student erred, and have the student look at
   the word and repeat your response.

think	pretty	light
five	better	would

better	light	five
pretty	would	think

would	five	better
think	light	pretty

Figure 6

Mimeographed Sheet Example 2
(Computation, Measurement, and Rule Application)

(*Note:* Since this type of instruction is not stimulus-response, the tutorial supervisor can generate, or have the tutors generate, problems similar to those indicated as incorrect on the pretest. However, remember that the instruction always begins with the more simple items and moves eventually to those more complex, just as the pretest should have been organized.)

Long Division

(Tutor Instructions)

1. Point to one of the problems and ask your student, "Can you solve this problem?" If he or she can't, then go through the steps necessary to correctly solve the problem, explaining each step carefully. When you have arrived at the correct answer, say "I want you to go through the same steps that I did and explain what you are to do in each step." If the student completes the explanations and the problem correctly, then praise him or her and go on to the next problem. If the student cannot complete the explanation or the answer, carefully repeat the steps in correctly solving the problem, and then have the student once again repeat your example. Once it is finally correct, praise him or her and go on to the next problem. If the student can initially correctly solve the problem without your assistance, praise him or her, and then go on to the next problem.
2. Repeat step number 1 in solving the next problem, and so on.
3. Since the problems you will be working on from each mimeo or prepared sheet are essentially the same with different numbers, the student will sooner or later discover that if the process works in correctly solving the first problem, it will also work for the other problems. Thus, it is essential to explain each step carefully in solving the problem.

1. $327\overline{)5,318}$ 2. $675\overline{)9,843}$ 3. $419\overline{)8,213}$

4. $192\overline{)7,351}$ 5. $784\overline{)9,129}$ 6. $245\overline{)4,733}$

(Continued on Next Page)

Figure 6 (Continued)

Steps to Solving the Problem. (Tutor can write the steps down as they are explained. The student can then refer to the steps as he or she is explaining the steps back to the tutor.)

    1.

    2.

    3.

    4.

    5.

    6.

Figure 7

Flash Card Example
(Stimulus-Response)

(*Note:* It will be to everyone's benefit if the tutor learns first The Flash Card Technique before trying any "real world" instruction with students. Thus, the stimulus-response example which follows will incorporate this technique.

Sight Words

1. Prepare the Flash Cards
If you can use printed flash cards that you purchased, you will be much better off. However, if you can't or don't have the resources to do it, give heed to these suggestions.
    (a)   On 3 x 5 flash cards, print the letters, words, or numbers (the stimulus items) on one face of the card with a black felt pen.
    (b)   Make at least three (3) copies of each card per tutor.
    (c)   Cut off the upper right corner of each card to aid you in keeping the cards right side up and in order.

```
 _____
|               \
|               |
| think         |
|_____|
```

    (d)   If making letters, all should be lower case.
    (e)   Locate enough files or shoe boxes to store each tutor's cards.
    (f)   Organize the cards with index cards, or separate each stimuli set with a colored 3 x 5 card with no corners cut off.

2. How to Tutor Using the Flash Card Technique:
Step I—Rehearsal
    (a)   Place one flash card in a stack for each new stimulus you are teaching the student.
    (b)   Hold up one flash card at a time and tell the student the correct response to the stimulus on the card. (Example:

(Continued on Next Page)

Figure 7 (Continued)

"This sight word is 'think.' Can you say 'think'?") Note: Make certain the student is looking at the flash card as he or she repeats the answer.

(c) Each time the student repeats the correct answer, say "That is fine" or "Very good."

(d) If the student repeats the answer incorrectly, don't say "No" or "That's wrong." Tell the student the correct answer and have him or her repeat it back to you loud enough so you can hear it clearly.

(e) Require the student to repeat the answers at a rate of about one per second. This will keep him or her attentive.

(f) Begin to challenge the student to say the stimulus as fast as possible. You might even make it sort of a game of speed—who can say the stimulus first. Kids love this game.

Step II—Learning Check

Following the student's rehearsal of the six stimuli, tell him or her, "You have been doing very well. Now we are going to try something different."

(a) Place one flash card for each stimulus you have been rehearsing and say, "I want you to tell me the correct answer on each of these flash cards, okay?"

(b) *DO NOT* give the student any specific feedback on any of his or her responses during the learning check.

(c) Hold up one flash card at a time.

(d) Following the student's answers, place the correctly answered cards *face up* on the table in front of the student, and the hesitantly and/or incorrectly answered cards *face down* in front of yourself.

(e) If the student has given *at least two* correct responses, go on to the next step. If the student has not learned at least two answers, have him or her repeat the procedures outlined in step number I until at least two answers are obtained on the learning check.

(f) Remember to praise the student following the learning check.

Step III—Teaching the Remaining Answers

Following the learning check, the procedures below will teach the student the remaining answers.

(Continued on Next Page)

Figure 7 (Continued)

(a) Place the flash cards the student correctly responded to in a stack.

(b) Place three (3) flash cards of one (1) stimulus the student did not correctly respond to during the learning check (Example: Three flash cards of the word "think") and combine them with the stack of cards the student answered correctly.

(c) Mix the flash cards up and make certain the *first flash card on the stack is one the student knows.* It is important that the student begins the task successfully, at least on the first response.

(d) Tell the student, "When I hold up a flash card, you tell me what it says. This time I will tell you the answer, if you need help, okay?"

(e) Show the student one flash card at a time.

(f) If the student answers correctly, say "Very good," or "That's correct," then go on to the next card.

(g) If the student hesitated more than *one second,* give the correct answer and then have the student repeat it. If the student repeats it correctly, praise him or her, and then go on to the next flash card.

(h) If the student answers incorrectly, do not say "No." Simply give the correct answer and have the student repeat it.

(i) Require the student to repeat the answers at a rate of about *one per second.* This will keep him or her attentive.

(j) As the student increases in proficiency, praise him or her. *Be sure to speak up when giving praise.* The effectiveness of praise is lost if you mumble or speak too low.

(k) Once the student is able to correctly answer the stimulus on each flash card, continue to speed drill for a few minutes. Following this, teach the student the remaining new stimuli.

(l) Follow the procedures for teaching the second new stimulus:
1. Remove from the stack one (1) of the three flash cards for the new stimuli just learned (e.g., think).
2. Add three (3) of a new stimulus the student does not know as determined from the learning check.

(Continued on Next Page)

Figure 7 (Continued)

    3.   Follow the same procedures as you followed for teaching the first new stimulus.

(m) Continue the drill until the student can correctly answer, without hesitation, the new stimulus. Drill for a few minutes more. When you feel the student is ready, follow the procedures below for teaching the third new stimulus.

    1.   Remove from the stack, one (1) more of the flash cards for the first new stimulus. This should leave one (1) flash card of the first newly learned stimulus in the stack.

    2.   Remove one (1) of the three (3) flash cards for the second stimulus taught. There should now be two (2) cards of the second stimulus in the stack.

    3.   Add three (3) flash cards for the third stimulus to be taught, as determined from the learning check.

    4.   Follow the drill procedures for teaching the first new stimulus.

(n) If there are additional new stimuli to be learned, continue to retain one flash card for each stimulus the student knew before the last stimulus was introduced, and three flash cards for the latest new stimulus being introduced.

Note: If you find the student consistently has trouble answering correctly for one or more of the new stimuli introduced in previous sessions, *do not* introduce a new stimulus until the student is able to answer in *two successive sessions for each flash card.*

(o) Remember, it is your responsibility as the tutor to make your student feel good about being tutored. It is, therefore, very important that you tell the student at the end of each session that he or she has done well, and that you are proud of him or her.

Figure 8

Flash Card Example
(Computation, Measurement, and Rule Application)

(*Note:* The Flash Card Technique is not especially applicable to higher order tutorial tasks. Thus, some new instructional procedures will be outlined, and then a few tasks will be given as examples.)

(Tutor Instructions)
1. Tell the student the task on which you are going to be working (e.g., "We are going to be working with the basic parts of speech.").
2. Explain to the student exactly what he or she is to do (e.g., "When I hold up a flash card, I want you to read the short sentence on the card, then identify all the parts of speech in the sentence.").
3. If the student cannot identify any of the parts of speech, it would be to the student's advantage to learn the parts of speech in a stimulus-response flash card program.
4. If the student can correctly identify some of the parts of speech in a given sentence, then you can go on to the next step.
5. The tutor should identify all the parts of speech, and then explain to the student why and how they are different from one another. The student is then asked to repeat the identification and essential explanations, *using his or her own words,* back to the tutor.
6. The tutor should never say "No" when the student is incorrect; instead, the tutor should just provide the correct answer *and* explain why it is the correct answer.
7. In most computation, measurement, and rule application problems, there are certain rules and/or procedures that when learned in one situation can be more easily understood and identified in new, similar situations. Thus, the problems you give your students in each tutorial session should be basically similar to one another. The march to greater complexity should be a gradual one.

Examples:
    (1) Flash cards containing instructions to measure various objects using a metric measuring tape.
    (2) Flash cards with computation formulas or problems for the student to solve.
    (3) Flash cards containing various specific examples of rules that the student is to identify and explain.
    (4) Flash cards containing rules for which the student is to supply appropriate examples.

6. Designing a Tutor Log and Tutor Assignment Sheet

The most common Tutor Log design is simple, yet provides enough structure to give very informative information concerning the activities and interactions between tutor and student. It should be an open-ended design. This type of log, however, requires a fair amount of writing skill on the part of the peer tutor.

The tutor should record entries into the Log following each tutorial session. They can be as detailed or as brief as the supervisor desires.

Tutor Log Construction

The design of the Tutor Log should be simple and easy to understand. A good Tutor Log will have at least the following items:

> (1) a place to record the name, age, and grade of both the tutor and student;
>
> (2) a place to record the date and time of each tutorial session;
>
> (3) a place to record the tutorial activity; and
>
> (4) a place to record the tutor's comments regarding the student's progress or lack of it.

The date and time of the tutorial session are first recorded, then a detailed description should be given of the specific activities which took place during the session. The last column is for comments about the student's progress during the session.

The design of the Tutor Assignment Sheet should also be easy to understand. It should also have at least the following items:

> (1) a place to record the name, grade, and teacher of the tutor;
>
> (2) a place to record the date;
>
> (3) a place to record the name, grade, and classroom teacher of the tutee;
>
> (4) a place to record the nature of the specific tutorial assignments; and

(5) a place to record the specific time, dates, and location of the tutorial sessions.

Two examples of a Tutor Log (Figures 9 and 10) and one example of a Tutor Assignment Sheet (Figure 11) follow.

(Text Continued on Page 67)

Figure 9

Tutor Log

Name of Tutor ...., Age/Grade ...., Teacher ....

Name of Student ...., Age/Grade ...., Teacher ....

Date and Time	Tutorial Activity	Comments

Figure 10

Tutor Log

Name of Tutor ...., Age/Grade ...., Teacher ....

Name of Student ...., Age/Grade ...., Teacher ....

Date and Time	Tutorial Activity	Achievement
9/29/79	Worked on correct answers [✓]	Student learned new answers [ ]
	Learning check [✓]	Student learned the following new answers: 532, 6,278
	Learned new answers [ ]	Did the student work well today? [ ]
	New answer target: 532, 6,278, 19,430	
9/30/79	Worked on correct answers [ ]	Student learned new answers [ ]
	Learning check [ ]	Student learned the following new answers:
	Learned new answers [ ]	Did the student work well today? [ ]
	New answer target:	

Figure 11

Tutor Assignment Sheet

Date ....

Tutor ...., Grade ...., Teacher ....

You are assigned to tutor ....

a .... grade student in .... 's

classroom, room number ....

You are to tutor the student on the following items: ....

. ...

. ...

. ...

You will tutor on the following days: ....

. ..., at .... in room ....

Report to your supervisor and bring your Tutor Log when you

feel the student has learned what you were directed to teach.

7. Determining the Tutorial Group Size

There are no particular examples which are appropriate here. The important thing to remember is to begin your peer tutorial program on a one-to-one basis, branching out only if the tutors and students can handle it.

8. Selecting and Training Peer Tutors

In a large sense, the success of your program depends upon how well you select and train your peer tutors. In the previous chapter, specific information was given of which you, as the supervisor, need to be well aware. It would be good to review that chapter, especially before you select anyone for your program.

It is highly recommended that you first select only ten to 12 tutors. Any more will reduce your effectiveness as a supervisor. Select an even number of tutors, since they will be working in pairs during their training.

It is best to have four training sessions. Each session will be important, so be highly organized before you begin your training. The training sessions should consist of the following.

Training Session #1
1. Instruction and practice on introductory techniques.
2. Instruction and practice on general tutoring procedures.

Training Session #2
3. Instruction and practice on pretesting and posttesting procedures.
4. Practice in filling out the Student Record Forms.

Training Session #3
5. Instruction and practice on tutoring from the instructional materials.
6. Practice in filling out the Tutor Log.

Training Session #4
7. Instruction and practice in determining the instructional assignments and reviews.

8. Practice in filling out the Summative Learning Gains Record.

An important thing to remember is that when you, as the supervisor, are instructing your tutors in each of the training sessions, it is best to first *explain the procedure or technique, then demonstrate it,* and *then have the tutors practice through role-playing.*

To further help you set up your training sessions, each of the eight topics will be briefly outlined below.

(1) Introductory Techniques

It has been found that when younger children are taken out of their regular classroom to be tutored, they are often tense and afraid. It is, thus, quite imperative that each student (tutee) be put at ease at the beginning of each tutoring session, especially the first.

The following techniques are suggestions of known successful practices. Instruct your tutors on these techniques. Then, have them pair off and practice by role-playing, with each tutor playing the role of *both* the tutor and student.

Use with Primary Grade Students:

"Hi, my name is . . . . What is your name?"

"Do you like pets?" (Talk briefly about pets.)

"Do you like to play games?"

"We are going to be playing some fun games today."

"Will you try to do the very best you can when we play some of these games?"

Use with Older Students:

"Hi there, my name is . . . . What's yours?"

"What are your favorite subjects in school?" *or*

"What do you like to do after school?" *or*

"What sports do you like?"

(Talk briefly, then explain you will be working closely together in the next few weeks and that there are a lot of things you both will be learning.)

Tell the student, regardless of grade level, to be sure to attend all tutoring sessions and to be on time when the sessions are scheduled.

(2) General Tutoring Procedures

Instruction and practice should be given to all tutors on each of the following tutorial procedures. Following instruction, have all the tutors pair off and role-play, with each tutor playing the role of *both* the tutor and student.

(a) *Work consistently with the student. You should meet a minimum of three times per week in order to insure success.* Meeting any less can greatly reduce the effectiveness of the tutorial technique.

(b) *Encourage and praise the student consistently.* There are few things, if any, which will motivate children as well as praise, when appropriately given. Also, in order for the praise to remain effective, it should be varied from time to time. Don't use the same phrases all the time.

(c) When the student does not give the correct response, or if he or she hesitates too long during instruction, not during the learning check, *tell him or her the correct response and then have him or her repeat it back to you.* Make sure that the student looks at the stimulus-response items. Just give the correct response, and have the student repeat it.

(d) *Avoid negative or punishing behavior.* Don't say "No" or convey displeasure, either verbally or facially, when the student gives an incorrect response. Try to be positive at all times.

(e) If the student is just not "catching on," *don't hesitate to clarify the task* even to the extent of demonstrating again and again.

(f) *Maintain accurate records of the student's progress.* Keep the Student Record Form and Tutor Log

up-to-date by making appropriate entries following
each tutorial session.

(g) *When tutoring your student, sit side-by-side* rather
than facing each other in a confrontation-type
position.

(h) *The use of the contingencies may be a helpful way
of increasing student motivation;* however, be realis-
tic in setting up the type of reward, the time span,
and the demonstrated behavior necessary to receive
the reward.

(i) *When working with young children, remember that
when they experience success, they will tolerate a
lot of necessary drill and practice.* However, young
children do not have attention spans of much
beyond 15 to 20 minutes at a time. Also, if taught
too many things in too short a period of time, they
will become confused. *Mastery and practice are
critical* before teaching new stimuli to young
children.

(j) *Above all, you as the tutor should be positive and
as happy as possible when working with your
student.* Also, be patient. Not all students are as
capable as others; thus, you may need to drill a lot
before learning takes place.

(3) Pretesting and Posttesting Procedures

The supervisor should first instruct the tutors by explaining the testing procedures, then demonstrating them, and
then having the students practice through role-playing. Each
tutor should have a sample or work copy of at least the
pretest to work with during role-playing.

Your instruction, of course, will depend upon the type of
pretest you develop. Be sure to check carefully that each
tutor is able to pretest well before going on to the next item
of instruction.

(4) Filling Out the Student Record Forms

First, the supervisor should explain the procedures for accurately filling out the Student Record Form following administration of the pretest. Second, the supervisor should demonstrate how this is done, being careful to observe if all tutors are attentive and completely understand the procedures. Lastly, the tutors should role-play by filling out sample Student Record Forms.

Again, the supervisor should closely observe that all tutors are competent in transferring the pretest information accurately on to the Student Record Form.

(5) Tutoring from the Instructional Materials

Instruction in this area will most likely be longer and more involved than in previous or subsequent training sessions. Thus, be sure to plan well and decide early which type of materials to use and the instructional level in which your tutors will tutor, i.e., the flash cards or the mimeo sheets at stimulus-response or higher cognitive levels.

The training format should follow the *explanation, demonstration,* and *practice* model. Do not begin additional instruction until all tutors have demonstrated mastery of the techniques and procedures involved in this training session. To insure this, you may have to allow additional time for practice.

(6) Filling Out the Tutor Log

This topic is the least demanding of all eight. The only instruction necessary is to first prepare sample Tutor Log pages, demonstrate how they can or should be filled out, and then require the tutors to practice for a short while.

(7) Determining the Instructional Assignments and Reviews

If you, as the supervisor, decide to handle all the instructional assignments and schedule reviews yourself, then no instruction on this topic for your tutors is necessary. If you want the peer tutors to make these decisions, then you probably should instruct your tutors carefully on the following items:

(a) determining how many stimuli the student can adequately handle during each tutorial session;

(b) determining when mastery has been obtained; and

(c) determining how often reviews should be given.

Specific suggestions on each of the three above items are found earlier in this "Design Format" chapter and in the "Operational Description" chapter. You may, however, find that more flexibility is needed. If so, don't hesitate to make the necessary changes.

(8) Filling Out the Summative Learning Gains Record

In order to more thoroughly instruct on this topic, you, as the supervisor, should have sample copies of both a pretest and posttest already filled out. The task for the peer tutors is to subtract pretest section scores from posttest section scores, thus coming up with specific and sectional learning gain scores. The peer tutors then post these scores on a sample Summative Learning Gains Record.

Again, the *explanation, demonstration,* and *practice* model should be used.

Note: Following each training session, the peer tutors should be praised and encouraged. You might even devise some type of achievement certificate to be issued to all those peer tutors successfully completing all tutorial training sessions. Young tutors will work hard for these certificates, if told about them in advance of their training.

9. Determining Instructional Assignments and Reviews

Since sufficient specific information was given on this topic in the last section, on the selecting and training of peer tutors, there is no need to repeat it here.

10. Designing a Posttest and a Summative Learning Gains Record

The posttest used following instruction can be the same instrument as the pretest. However, be sure that adequate time has passed, i.e., several weeks or months of instruction, so that memory of specific pretest item responses has extinguished. If you are in doubt about an adequate length of time, then design a new posttest, but make it as parallel as possible to the pretest.

The procedures used in posttesting should be identical to those used in pretesting. However, if you plan to collect data on your program, and by all means you should, your data will be more reliable if someone other than the assigned peer tutor does the posttesting. Young tutors posttesting their own students sometimes have a tendency to cue and give hints to their students in anticipation of high posttest scores. A new person conducting the posttest will insure that the tutee is given a proper and fair evaluation. Do, however, encourage a friendly introduction of the tutee and the new posttester prior to (i.e., a week or a few days) the actual posttest. This will reduce anxiety and other inhibiting factors that often work on a young student when faced with a new person in a testing situation.

The design of the Summative Learning Gains Record is quite simple as long as you keep the following thought in mind. The purpose of the Record is to record the differences in performance between the pretest and the posttest. Its design, then, is open as long as it accomplishes the stated purpose.

Summative Learning Gains Record Construction

The posttest can be constructed exactly like the pretest *if* there is a considerable period of time, i.e., several weeks or months, between pretest and posttest. If, however, there is a good chance that tutees will remember the specific pretest stimuli, design a *closely parallel* posttest.

The Summative Learning Gains Record is easy to construct. The following items, however, should be included:

    (1) a place to record the student's name, age, grade, and school;

    (2) a place to record the name and age of the tutor;

(3) a place to record the number of weeks the student was tutored;

(4) a place to record the number of tutorial sessions the student attended;

(5) a place to record the average number of minutes each tutorial session lasted;

(6) a place to record the total instructional time in hours and minutes;

(7) a place to record the date the pretest was administered and the name of the person administering the pretest;

(8) a place to record the date the posttest was administered and the name of the person administering the posttest;

(9) places to record the number of correct responses, per stimuli group, when pretested;

(10) places to record the number of correct responses, per stimuli group, when posttested;

(11) places to record the overall gain from pretest to posttest for each stimuli group; and

(12) a place for comments.

An example of determining learning gains would be if a student correctly responded to 20 stimulus-response items on the pretest and 45 items on the posttest; the learning gain would be +25. If, however, the student correctly responded to 20 items on the pretest and only 15 on the posttest, the learning "gain" is -5.

See Figure 12 for an example of a Summative Learning Gains Record which is adaptable for just about any type of objective in which someone tutors another. Figure 13 is a sample Summative Learning Gains Record used in reading. It is so organized to be filled in.

(Text Continued on Page 78)

Figure 12

·Summative Learning Gains Record

Student .... Age ....

School .... Grade ....

Tutor .... Age ....

School .... Grade ....

The student was tutored for .... weeks.
The student was tutored a total of .... times.
On the average, the tutoring session lasted .... minutes.
Total instructional time .... hours .... minutes.

Objective tutored on: ....

....

Pretest date .... Pretested by ....

(On the following, use as many lines as necessary to record completely the pretest information.)

When pretested, the student knew .... of .... possible ....
(Fill in appropriate description, such as problems, examples.)

Posttest date .... Posttested by ....

When posttested, the student knew .... of .... possible ....

The student learned (fill in appropriate description):

Comments:

Figure 13

Summative Learning Gains Record

Student .... Age ....

School .... Grade ....

Tutor .... Age ....

School .... Grade ....

The student was tutored for .... weeks.
The student was tutored a total of .... times.
On the average, the tutoring session lasted .... minutes.
Total instructional time .... hours .... minutes.
Objective tutored on: ....

Pretest date .... Pretested by ....

When pretested, the student knew .... of 26 letter names.
When pretested, the student knew .... of 20 consonant sounds.
When pretested, the student knew .... short vowel sounds.
When pretested, the student knew .... of eight digraph sounds.
When pretested, the student knew .... of 23 basic sight words.
When pretested, the student knew .... of the 148 additional sight words.
When pretested, the student was able to read .... of the ....
nonsense words.

Posttest date .... Posttested by ....

When posttested, the student knew .... of 26 letter names.
When posttested, the student knew .... of 20 consonant sounds.
When posttested, the student knew .... short vowel sounds.
When posttested, the student knew .... of eight digraph sounds.
When posttested, the student knew .... of 23 basic sight words.
When posttested, the student knew .... of the 148 additional sight words.
When posttested, the student was able to read .... of the ....
nonsense words.

(Continued on Next Page)

Figure 13 (Continued)

The student learned .... letter names.
The student learned .... consonant sounds.
The student learned .... short vowel sounds.
The student learned .... digraph sounds.
The student learned a total of .... sight words.
The student read .... more nonsense words on the posttest than read on the pretest.

Comments:

11. Developing a Schedule for the Peer Tutors

In scheduling tutorial sessions, it is often as easy to schedule several tutorial pairs as it is to schedule a few. There is no ideal number of tutorial pairs to schedule in the same location, as long as each peer tutor and assigned tutee are able to work together without distraction. However, if nothing else, the space available in your assigned location may determine how many tutorial pairs you can have operating at one time.

Since there are no suggested examples or schedule designs appropriate for this topic, it might be well to repeat a critical point made in the "Operational Description" chapter. To insure that your peer tutorial program succeeds and that significant learning gains are made, *the tutor and student should work together at least three times per week at least 15 or 20 minutes per session.*

12. Monitoring the Peer Tutors and the Tutorial System

Probably the most important thing to do when monitoring either your tutors or system is to carefully evaluate if your stated objectives are being met. If they are not, then changes in the objectives, tutors, or system should be made. Also of great importance is to observe if the tutors are carefully following your instructional procedures. If they are not, then changes in the tutors or procedures should be made.

An interesting thought not mentioned previously would be to randomly select a few peer tutors to monitor closely their own cognitive and affective gains following tutorial involvement. This may be accomplished through pretesting and posttesting procedures using more advanced test instruments than those designed for the students. There is a definite need for additional research on the cognitive and affective growth of tutors involved in well-constructed and implemented peer tutorial programs. In a closely monitored system, there should be few problems in conducting this type of research.

Figures 14 and 15 can be of assistance in monitoring your objectives and tutors.

Figure 14

Objective Monitor Form

Objectives	Are Being Accomplished	Not Being Accomplished	Comments

Figure 15

Tutor Monitor Form

Tutors	Are Following the Procedures	Not Following the Procedures	Comments

IV.

OUTCOMES

The emphasis throughout this book has been on the administrator and/or teacher. Procedures have been provided for setting up a peer tutorial program. The benefits of a well-designed and implemented program are many. The following is a summary of these benefits:

1. The Peer Tutorial Instruction approach objectifies and structures the learning process. The creation of specific objectives is an integral part of the program. These objectives are evaluated to see if they are specifically accomplished by both the peer tutors and learners following the tutorial involvement. This may seem like too much objectivity from the perspective of humanists; however, in remediation efforts, objective tutoring has no peer (excuse the pun). Carefully constructed objectives lead to a high degree of structure, leaving little or no room for deviation. If designed appropriately, this structure will insure success for those students who have so often experienced failure.

2. Another important function of peer tutorial instruction is the diagnostic assessment of the cognitive, affective, or psychomotor strengths and weaknesses of the learner. It is from these diagnoses that tutorial instruction begins to focus. Weak areas receive particular attention, and through mastery and review checks we are assured that these weak areas will become strengths.

3. Since success is a primary goal of a good peer tutorial program, adequate safeguards are usually built-in to insure this success. When previously failing youngsters begin experiencing success, positive self-concept development is enhanced. Also, since tutorial instruction demands communication for feedback purposes, those students who are shy or non-communicative often overcome these problems. Although these emotional advancements made by students are not easy to empirically demonstrate, they may, however, be more worthwhile and important than the cognitive development the students will experience.

4. The usually unanticipated cognitive and affective growth of the peer tutors is less discernible than the growth of the tutees, yet often the peer tutors actually experience greater growth. Although more research is needed in this area, there has been enough already to substantiate exceptional cognitive and affective growth on the part of peer tutors.

5. One of the more important advantages of a sound peer tutorial program is the help it renders the classroom teacher. Teachers who spend significant periods of time trying to remediate slow learners during regular class instruction find the above average students becoming unmotivated, unchallenged, and eventually unproductive. What peer tutoring can do is to challenge the above average students by selecting and training them as tutors. In addition, the slow students will have the unique opportunity to be tutored, which insures cognitive advancements that these students would not get in the regular classroom. Thus, the instruction during the regular classroom could be more efficient and effective for the rest of the students.

6. Another important advantage of a good, well-constructed peer tutorial program is the low cost involved and the ease with which it can be implemented. Since the cost of educational programs keeps increasing, it is refreshing to

know that there is an alternative instructional format that not only is effective, but also is low in cost. In fact, the only cost that is absolutely necessary is time—the time spent in developing the program. If the development is careful and you have courted your administrators and colleagues well, any type of peer tutorial program will be relatively easy to implement. Implementation takes cooperation.

V.

DEVELOPMENTAL GUIDE

While the development of a peer tutorial program is not difficult, it will take some time before you can implement your finished program. The majority of time will be devoted to formulating objectives and developing tests and forms outlined in the "Design Format" chapter.

Since the steps for developing your own program are explicitly outlined in both the "Operational Description" and "Design Format" chapters, only a checklist will be provided in this chapter. This checklist, however, should prove valuable to you in the development of your own peer tutorial program. See Figure 16.

The author will appreciate *any* sort of feedback from those who develop and implement their own peer tutorial programs based upon any of the suggestions offered in this book.

The author again wishes to acknowledge the pioneering work in Structured Tutoring by Grant Von Harrison at Brigham Young University. Without his efforts, many of the specifics in this book would not, in fact, be so specific.

Figure 16

Developmental Guide Checklist:
(Peer Tutorial Instruction)

STEPS	ACCOMPLISHED	
	No	Yes
1. Selection of the Learners		
2. Determine the Instructional Objectives		
3. Design the Diagnostic Pretests and Outlining Pretesting Procedures		
4. Develop Comprehensive Student Record Forms and Record-Keeping Procedures		
5. Develop and Structure the Instructional Materials		
6. Design a Tutor Log and Tutor Assignment Sheet		
7. Determine the Tutorial Group Size		
8. Selection and Training of Peer Tutors		
9. Determine the Instructional Assignments and Reviews		
10. Design a Posttest and a Summative Learning Gains Record		
11. Develop a Schedule for the Peer Tutors		
12. Monitoring the Peer Tutors and Tutorial System		

VI.

RESOURCES

Peer Tutorial Instruction is an old concept gaining new attention. Many of the ideas contained in this book are not original; however, this is an original attempt to put the various ideas together in one source.

Additional information may be obtained from the following sources.

BOOKS

Allen, Vernon L. (Editor) *Children as Teachers.* New York: Academic Press, 1976.

Harrison, Grant V. Beginning Reading 1, Beginning Reading 2, Basic Reading for Secondary Students, and Basic Reading for Adults. Department of Instructional Science, Brigham Young University, Provo, Utah, 1976.

Melaragno, Ralph J. *Tutoring with Students: A Handbook for Establishing Tutorial Programs in Schools.* Englewood Cliffs, New Jersey: Educational Technology Publications, 1976.

Endsley, William R. *The Effects of Rehearsal Task Structure and Orienting Instructions on Levels of Information Processing.* Unpublished doctoral dissertation, Department of Instructional Science, Brigham Young University, Provo, Utah, 1976.

WORKSHOPS

The author conducts one-day workshops on setting up peer tutorial programs: 8735 Avalon Street, Alta Loma, California 91701.

WILLIAM R. ENDSLEY completed graduate school at Brigham Young University in 1974, following four years of service as an Officer in the United States Army. Upon completion of graduate school, Dr. Endsley coordinated the undergraduate educational psychology program and taught and conducted research at Southern Illinois University at Carbondale. He is presently involved in the development and implementation of various training programs in Alta Loma, California and is developing a tutorial reading program for public use.